Through My Eyes

Seraphina Wong

Presentation by *BookLeaf Publishing*

Web: www.bookleafpub.com

E-mail: info@bookleafpub.com

ISBN: 9789357748315

First edition 2023

DEDICATION

To the one who believes in me even when I can't
believe in myself: Thank you, God.

Guardians

in an ambiance of red and blue
a tawny yellow for a backdrop
only in its presence when asleep
does the dragon keep watch
over its ward.
sheltered by the blankets
the bed sends her off to the dreamworld
where chaos, as always,
awaits her.
as she tosses and turns
encountering twisted memories
and longed for adventures
the room hums
hoping that she will not
be disturbed.
the stars hold their breath
the moon brushes her hair
the clock quiets its tick
the sun slowly peeks through
careful to only give warmth
until the time is right.
her return is sudden
but the flowers let out a sigh
of relief
she has slept through
the night
a rare occurrence in that
small child's life.

Fearfully and Wonderfully Made

He takes the first light of dawn
and places it in a newborn's eyes
He takes two delicate snowflakes
and watches them melt into her cheeks
He takes the first bud of spring
and colors her lips pink
He takes the gentle shine of the moon
and from it weaves her hair
He takes the loyalty of the mountains
and sings it in her heart
He takes the passion of the oceans
and hides it in her tears
He takes the strength of the highest oak tree
and carves it in her bones
He takes the playfulness of the wind
and paints it in her laugh
He takes the wisdom of the stars
and awakens her curious mind
He takes the grace of falling leaves
and blesses her tiny feet
He takes the brightness of the sun
and makes it her smile
He takes the warmth of the fire
and forges her embrace
He takes His breath
and breathes into her life
He takes His soul
and gifts her eternal love

Sunflowers

Unlike the sun, with all of its warmth
and its gift to create life
At best I am like a sunflower
doing its best to seem like sunshine
Rooted in the dirt, but with my head
always in the clouds
there's a stark difference between
the celestial and the terrestrial
But if there's one thing that
remains the same
it is the joy that just by being gives
See the smiles, see the love
realize that you share the
golden beauty of the sun

Burning Alive

When does passion
transform from a driving fuel
to all-consuming destruction?
What is the line between
doing your best
and going too far?
We all know the fear of failure,
but what about the fear of success?
In order to achieve your dreams,
what do you end up sacrificing?
Instead of joy, I feel anxious,
my mind flooded with thoughts
of ruining everything I created
with a single mistake.
Am I on fire for what I love,
or is what I love setting me on fire
In a way I can't control,
leaving me bleeding out on the ground,
choking on the ashes of the happiness
I thought I had found?

Lotus

Trapped in muddy anger,
resentment clinging to my skin
like a leech,
I do not know if it is rage
at the world
or at myself
that leaves me stuck
in the darkness.
The weight of hatred,
shame, and regret
is heavy, causing me to sink
even further beneath
these murky waters.
If my soul is that
of a lotus,
why, then, does the dirt
that stains my heart
not wash away?

Tired

I am tired of clinging to hope
when all that surrounds me is the wreckage
of what I once held dear.
I am tired of fighting for peace
when the voices in my head ring louder and louder
every time I try to resist.
I am tired of trying to be strong
when the world keeps bringing me to my knees
bloodied and broken.
I am tired of looking for joy
when every silver lining in the clouds
turns to ashes.
I am tired of yearning for love
when abandonment and anxiety are closer
than my own heartbeat.
I am tired of pretending I'm okay
when I'm falling apart piece by piece inside
and smiling hurts.
I am tired of these beautiful thoughts
when I'm in the midst of despair
that fill me with false promises.

Breathe

In
Out
Drown
In, Out, and
Still
I drown
Why am I
Choking on what is
Supposed to
Give me
Life
How much
Longer
Do I have to
Endure
All I
Want is to
Breathe
Easy again
Am I
Asking for
Too much?

Sandcastle

At the end of my sleeves lies a beach
embracing the waves flowing down my cheeks
the soft barrier between the ocean within
and the sandcastle I make my home in.

Still, it cannot stop the incoming tide
not even a grain is left behind
and I find myself slipping under clouds of salt
unlocking not a box, but Poseidon's vault.

I crash into a shore made of broken shells
the sea billows roar through my head like bells
a world of blur stings the corners of my eyes
until all I see are the stars in the sky.

Though I have crumbled, there is an empty peace
I will rebuild this home, piece by piece.

Broken Faith

I came to the well, certain that I
could draw a bucket full
but my arms were not strong enough.
A bowl, then, perhaps would suffice
yet still, my arms shook
and the bowl slipped out of my grasp.
A glass, this time, surely I
could drink from the well
but my grip, anxious, shattered
the vessel, and again no water was drawn.
In desperation, I dipped a cup
realizing too late the cracks.
Slumped against the side, with nothing
to use but my hands
the amount I could taste was minuscule.
But the water was sweet, full
of life, and finally, I knew
all I could offer were these two small hands.

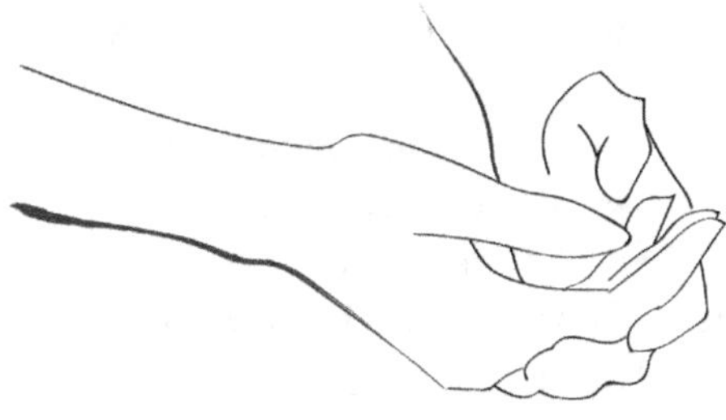

Little One

You who every evening would read stories
underneath the stars
You who smiled and dreamed so freely,
who sang songs of pure joy
You who played make-believe in forts made of
pillows and tables
Those beautiful days spent in innocent bliss,
when magic still
Twinkled in every object and action,
where did it all go?
The fearless curiosity of a child faded so
suddenly, the mind playing
make-believe in lonely cages
Scared by the stars that watched her,
their glow no longer welcoming
Her dreams of being a fire, a light, in the world
vanished
Except for in the back of her mind, where magic
still exists
That giant castle she spent her days
locked in was dark and cold
Until she could take no more and lit
a small candle, so small
Yet so warm
The dragon that had slumbered for so long awoke
You who were scared of the stars,
did you forget the light you were?
You are the prince, the princess, the dragon.
Live your fairytale.

When Dawn Breaks

Dark blue pierced and interrupted by sharp
angles and tips,
until slowly the colors start to shift and change,
from blue to purple to red to pink to orange,
blending together like a painting created
with a brush that could only go across
the canvas horizontally.
Then a small yet growing light rises,
obscured by the peaks and summits
of the unmoving,
still undaunted and steadfast in its glow,
until it overcomes the hostility and
softens the edges with golden white
kisses no thing could resist.
My eyes are wide, my body positioned
to be consumed completely by the awe and
wonder of the flames that dance and
call to my soul.
What is tired, what is pain, my limbs
have forgotten, and I find myself covered
in ink, in glass, in hope,
in the first words of a dying heart.

Broken Pottery

Broken pottery is still beautiful
The Potter takes the shattered pieces
And seals them together
With gold, leaving veins that shimmer
And an image of restoration
Perhaps all the pieces
Have yet to be put together
And sometimes you get cut
Picking them off the floor
But slowly and surely
A masterpiece is in the making
Your Creator will not leave you unfinished
You are meant to be a treasure.

Mei Hua

Underneath moonlit petals with a pale pink glow
Silver streams of peace stain my cracked lips.
Frozen hands and a beating heart are a reminder
That even in the dead of winter, life persists.

The white that can't be dyed with ink
Reflects the purity of a new beginning.
Let past and pain be swept away in the river
And let the unfamiliar emptiness sink in.

With every breath that scratches my lungs
Winter crafts a burning song in my soul.
I will carve a path of light in the darkness
Like a flower that blooms proudly in the snow.

From the Ashes

what you thought was
the end
was really just a
new beginning
for the fire that
burns within
cannot be put out
despite storms
despite suffocation
despite opposition
even when you feel
like all that is left of you
is ashes
there is still at least
one ember
alive
and for a
phoenix to
rise,
all it takes
is a single
spark

Moonchild

You look up in the night
In awe of the moon
Of its gentle yet brilliant light
I wonder if you realize
How similar you are
There are craters in your skin
From where the world has
Beaten and bruised and scarred you
Yet despite your wounds
Despite the hurt you have endured
Your smile is soft and your soul shines
Wisps of clouds, of tears,
Cause your eyes to see the world
In all of its mesmerizing colors
Stars dance across your cheeks
Kissing your nose
Your beauty twinkles in the day and night
Sometimes there are times
When your light is hidden from the world
Sometimes there are times
When your light illuminates the darkest spaces
When you are gone, you are missed
When you are present, you are cherished
In every phase a sight to behold
Beloved moonchild
I always love returning your embrace

4:14

the melody of your soul
is crafted around a single verse
"Perhaps this is the moment
for which you have been
created"
in that every moment
you exist in is why
you have been made
a blessing simply to be
a gift simply to know
and one day you will find
that moment
where every experience
every hurt, every joy
that you've gone through
leads up to
and you will bloom
your symphony ringing through
the stars
but whether it is
in that moment or
in every moment
your song burns bright
against the dark
each note captivating
creating harmonies
that even angels
are in awe of

A Divine Heir

They say that crowns and rings
are shackles in another form
That the gravity of their weight
is heavier than any cast-iron chain
After all, at least the cuff doesn't have
Expectations
Which means no
Disappointment
But though the burden exists, it is
Light, the expectations exist because
There is trust and belief
Belief in you
In the dark one can hide, but in the light
One can shine,
Freedom can only come from surrender
To a power that could but will never
Bind you against your will
Love and kingdom are your masters
Serving them will only lead to glory
So hold your head high
Stretch out your hand
You are worthy, beloved, an heir.

Descended From Dragons

Born in the year of the dragon
the immortal's blood runs through my veins
though I am far from the homeland.
There, dragons swim through the sky
bringers of water and life
images sculpted in jade and gold.
Here, dragons fall from the sky
breathers of fire and destruction
images carved in paper and steel.
And because I am here and not there
they try to cut my wings
to tame the monster that must live inside.
But I am from there and not here
I need no wings to fly
and an empress is who lives inside.

* 9 7 8 9 3 5 7 7 4 8 3 1 5 *